Poetic Encounter:
Rhapsodies from the South

Marota Aphane &
Oliver Mtapuri

Langaa Research & Publishing CIG
Mankon, Bamenda

Publisher
Langaa RPCIG
Langaa Research & Publishing Common Initiative Group
P.O. Box 902 Mankon
Bamenda
North West Region
Cameroon
Langaagrp@gmail.com
www.langaa-rpcig.net

Distributed in and outside N. America by African Books Collective
orders@africanbookscollective.com
www.africanbookscollective.com

ISBN-10: 9956-764-70-1

ISBN-13: 978-9956-764-70-9

About the Poets

Marota Aphane has Master of Development from the University of Limpopo (UL) and is currently works at University of Venda (UNIVEN), Directorate of Research and Innovation. As a poet, playwright and an academic he published both literary (poetry & plays) and academic works in national and international journals such as *New coin, Sweet magazine, Agenda, Kotatz, TurfWrite, Magic with Words, Systemic Practice Action Research, Journal of Education, Educational Research for Social Change, South African Medical Journal, Nonlinear Dynamics, Psychology, and Life Sciences, The Southern African Journal of Transdisciplinary Studies* etc.

Oliver Mtapuri is an Adjunct Professor at the University of Limpopo. He has a PhD in Development Studies from the University of KwaZulu Natal and an MBA degree from the University of Zimbabwe. He is an Associate of the Institute of Chartered Secretaries and Administrators. Oliver's areas of research interest include poverty, redistribution and inequality, community-based tourism, public employment programmes, research methodologies, financial management, climate change and project management. He writes poems, short stories and plays. Oliver also writes academic books particularly in Project Management and Entrepreneurship.

Poems by Marota Aphane

Kiba

(Pedi traditional dance)

In the beginning
A singing dance
Met a dancing song
And conceived
Kiba
The earth over flew
With ululating nectar

Then
The singing dance's
Voice
Grew hoarse
The dancing song's
Legs
Were crossed
In the no-sense
Of modern rust

And draught
Befell the earth.

Afrika

Beat the drums fast

Come all you

Warriors

Children of the besieged

Mother Afrika

Let's stump the ground hard

And raise the dust high

Let the dead know

It means war

That bloodstained

Obsolete monster

Santa

Still continues

Flooding and feeding

Our seedlings

With that barren poisonous

False taste

Coke

Let's ban the curser

Lest we perish.

Hlokatsebe

(one who doesn't listen)

Hlokatsebe

Use to be

A no barrier warrior

Of all ears

Without fears

Until he embarked

On a headless (chicken) mission

Without vision

Into the wilderness

Of the Hebrew fairy-tales.

Hlokatsebe

Is now a new-creature-preacher

Washed

By the blood of the *lionofjudahlamb*

A 'strue

Afrikan descendant of Jewish's ancestry?

Who spits phlegm

On the sacred ancestral poetry.

24/7

5

He barks about

Shoulders inflated

'Strue god!

I am African

Letter to masta

Dear masta

Every evening

Before you we congregate

We, the seedlings of our night coloured mother

masta

Before you, saw Seithlamo

We *'bend our third knees'*

And open our third ears

With our intellectual pockets bulging

Dear masta

But

Every evening

We scatter from you

Our heads aching hollow

From the collision

With your pop-bubble-gum-cult(ure)

masta

And here we are now

Mourning for the bosom blood

Succumbed to the poisonous so-called-soapes:

>*the bald and the bully-fools*
>
>*(dark) dyes of our (colourful) life*

the junk and taste-less

dull-us…

Forced down their intellectual throats

At the execution centres called lounge rooms

Masta

Here we are

Mumbling incoherent

Westerly ways without wealth

Gulped down from your long lousy lessons:

Lesson No. 1: Penguins who never dreamed of flying

Teaching us how to fly without wings

Elevated our spirits with the mythologies

Of their fermented myths

Innocently, smelling no rat

We rocketed

A hundred feet altitude

masta! masta!

We have a problem, over!

(no response)

masta! masta!

You forgot to wing us, over!

(no respond)

masta! masta!

Like shot down swallows
We crushed down head on
Masta
Now we are the retards.

Lesson No. 2: An alligator without a proper identity
>*"This lesson is meant to teach a lesson*
>*To all those who learnt less lesson*
>*From the first life-long lesson*
>*Feel free, come en masse to swim*
>*The crocs have taken a long leave"*

Innocently, suspecting nothing
We dived-deep into your sparkling-intoxicating-waters
And despised our looks since then.

Lesson No. 3: Hallucinating masta
>*You made funny blinding faces and deafening noises masta*

*THEN THE VOICE OF REASON FROM THE GRAY-
HAIRED WELLS OF WISDOM WE DESEATED AT
THE HEATH CALLED*
Lesson No. 4: The genuine lesson
>*My children's children*
>*This is the real lesson*

Penguins can't fly, penguins can't teach you how to fly
My children's children
Blood is thicker than water, alligators are close relatives of crocs
My children's children
This is the real lesson
White doesn't mean bright and Black doesn't mean bleak

So masta
It is with heartfelt great joy
That I have to spit on your face
And turn you off for good
As Jimmy Cliff rejoiced:
"I can see clearly now the rain is gone"

Yours truly
Retired serve-end
Wezindebe *(one with ears)*

The (t) rain will come

(Extract from the play:

"The Wait" by the same author)

Every sunrise

We wake our empty stomach

Hope (fool)

Today is different

The (t) rain will come

Twenty winters withered

Heads in collision

Our fed-up stomach still

Chants empty revolt-illusion

As the people's regiment fire

The same stinking fart

In unison

Today is today

The (t) rain will come

Every sundown

We sleep our empty stomach

Hope (fool)

Tomorrow is different

The (t) rain will come

I am South Afrikan

(Responding to Pres. Thabo Mbeki's
I am an African- conceptualised by Charity Sehlapelo)

By the complexion of my skin

That camouflages

With char-coal colour

The source of warmth

For my forgotten cross-tools people

I swear

I am South Afrikan

As the sun wakes

And wearily breaks

Wakes, breaks…

And the empty tri-pot bottom burns

For naught

With twig-kids

Twirling ritually around it

Hoping to calm the storm

Inside their desert tummies

My Baobab-Bark-Burned face wrinkles

Are polished and perfected

By the barrowing

Punched on my mother's stomach aiding to suck dry

Her wealthy blood to irrigate the world ceaselessly

From the Worst to the Yeast

I am not ashamed

To shout my bile out

I am a starving South Afrikan

All day

All day
I wait my head
Heavily
Balanced
On my knees

All day
I wait,
Hungry and angry
For the love of my neighbour
But, dear god
It doesn't
Come!

Then I go to sleep
With my stomach
Empty
Fed up
Yet
All night
My neighbour's words
Echoes

In my ears:

"Love your neighbour
As you love yourself"
All nightlong
Her words
Torment me
"Love…
Neighbour…
Yourself"
But, dear god
It doesn't
Come!

Our big black pot

My Lord!

In a round sloping earth

There is a green warm continent

In the green warm continent

There are wealthy generous lands

In the wealthy generous lands

There are gentle black people

In the gentle black people

There is an old deserted question

My Lord, we cry

We cry

With hollow stomach

As our big black pot

Is put on fire

We cry, we cry

As our big black pot

Is on cook

We cry, we cry

As our big black pot

Is ripen

We cry, we cry

As they feed from our big black pot

We cry, we cry

My Lord

Why, our big black pot

No longer feeds us all?

Donkey cry

(Responding to Maahlamela's pain)

We are tied

We are tired

We labour

30 hours a day

To reap whips

We are tied

We are tired

We labour

Oog-klapped (*donkey blinder*)

Never to see

Our brothers and sisters

On the roadsides

Shot dead

For free drinking

Their fountain water

For sale

We are tied

We are tired

We labour

Lips sealed

As they feed sweet

From the sweat of our dried brows

And we creep and crawl

To pick-up crumbs

Of the fruits of our labour

We are tied

We are tired

We labour

30 hours a day

To reap weeps

Today

We lay down the yoke

Our diligent hands

Aren't for sale

Mantlapulele *(celebrating rain)*

Bra Fani, the last time we met

Trees where dry

With no sign of life

And the wells were empty

Leaving us all thirst

All the time

This time we meet again

With nothing to gain

The trees are still naked

The wells are still dry

And we are still sweating

But, Bra Fani

Please tell me why our lives

Are always blue

I ask you, Bra Fani

Because you learned something

From the big books

On how to create joy

I ask you

Because I want you to know

Only god makes it rain

In the deep desert

So Bra Fani

In our lives god will make it

Rain one day

Then me and you

Shall sing and dance

Our childhood songs

Mantlapulele

Ballard of the daffodils

(For my parents)

I cleared a patch of land
Filled it with roses assorted
To fill my life with colour
And intoxicate the dull air with fragrance

I prayed and poured
From the depth of my heart
The living water on my rose garden
And waited wearily
To see seedlings breaking the ground
Of my mournful past

My stream of joy
Was filled to the brim
To see my fragile seedlings germinating

I summoned all the energies within
Fed and fenced my roses
With the muscles and veins of my heart
To fortify and shed them from all elements
But my heart broke still to watch

My future filled field
Withers before my tearful eyes

I gathered the last strength
And inhaled the fresh breath
Continue feeding and watering
Fragrance of colours for my tomorrow
Yet they lost their grip
On the fertile ground
Pregnant with life in abundance
And my heart staggered

With a mourning heart
I lovingly buried
My rose under the earth
And filled it with the daffodils
Passionately watered them
With the memories of my weathered roses

Then I set back
And watched with wander
As they grew
With a rampant colours
Of a beautiful life tomorrow

Then I knew

Oh, goodness

This earth's for daffodils!

To be bird

So, you thought
It will be easy
To have wings
And fly all your ways
Without a little
Fall on a thorny tree lesson?

So, you thought
It will be easy
To master flying
Without flipping wings
And dark the rain
Of mask-man's pellets
And never be grounded?

So, you thought
It will be easy
To return to the nest
Without a gale
To cut through?

So, you thought

It will be easy

To be bird

Little bird?

Nja tša satane *(evil dogs)*

They chased
The law-abiding lamb
In the field
Down the streams
Up the hills
Nja tša satane
Who failed to catch
The goats
That stole the corn.

The lamb was cornered
Strapped naked
Devoured
With red eyes burning hatred
And panting death-for-certain
They vanished.

How much she ran
How much the law stared her down.

She uttered a word
And one of the them,

The law suffering from incurable verbal-diarrhoea

Poured rotten words

On her confused head

And pierced her heart with sharp-needled-laughter

Leaving her bloody-wet

And gasping for breath,

The law-abiding lamb left

Feeling light like a feather.

Nja tša satane

They thought

She is finished

But her heart remained

Beating… and beating… and beating…

Hope

The dusk was dawning
Her tender feed were weary
Of fighting an endless
Unconquerable sand mirage
Tantalising
Her trusting sunken eyes
And dry throat
With pure pond water in a forever
Short distance
All day long.

Her usual short
Five walk case
For fire-wood
Became six...seven...
...ten her age
Seemed ancient

Then the night wolf
Came earlier
Dressed in a sheep's skins
And armed with well trained

Fork tongues

That promises

Light to any lost lamb

But gives wilderness

That darkens bright lamps

Her purple rose

Was filmed all night long

But her shaking strength

Tightened seconds to second

Boledi!

(for my wife, Mokgaetši: Short and Sweet)

For your kinky hair-style bold heart-shaped face calmly
flowing
like majestic Limpopo contended the jewel of Afrika's bowels
abducted kicked and kissed against your will my dimpled
melon sweet and short Hear please the only thirst
quenching droplet my desert lips offer
to eternity **You** and **Me**
shall forever remain
Nail and Finger!

You blinded

Come! Come walk with me
In the landscape of my weeping heart

Come see with me
The undulating Mount-Everest-s
Miseries of social-stigmas
I shoulder all dawns to dusks

Come taste with me
My sour meandering streams of tears that never
Waters the ground even in the ugliest-bluest-moons

Hush! Hush!
Hear those stinking hoots of owls from the night-turned-side
Cursing my woman-hood?

Come. Oh! come feel with me
The sole island woman of ancient tender rocks
That never melts to the million scorching suns

You blinded!
Come walk with me in the landscape of my weeping heart.

Revival

(for my late grandmother)

A caring gentle-lady

In the dusk

Of her lonely life

Relaxes and sew together

Tattered rags

Of our nearly destructed story

That the future

Won't catch cold

WHILST…

(for the late prof. J. Ruganda)

A diligent gentle-man

In the dusk

Of his struggling life

Is busy curving out

The almost deformed features

Of a bold black African face

That the future

Won't be confused.

Poems by Oliver Mtapuri

Ode to Nelson Mandela

(Written December 2013)

Our icon, our true hero

An African warrior

Without borders

Born in 1918.

You believed

You conceived

Love and peace.

You inspired

Son of the soil

A voice of reason

Hunted, arrested and charged for treason.

You fought for justice and peace

You preached reconciliation

Long before the wounds of apart-hate were healed.

Freedom for all is all you asked for……

You taught us everlasting lessons of life;

Selflessness, Mandela-ness

You dreamed
You imagined
A rainbow nation

You laid the values for the present and future
You are an embodiment of forgiveness
Your story will be told today and be re-told for forever;
Son of the soil
A stalwart and struggle hero
A gallant fighter

You fought and espoused the cause of the people to the end
Across borders and boundaries, you touched lives and the
hearts of all
Now we know, you liberated both the oppressed and the
oppressors
Nelson Rolihalhla Mandela.

You radiated magnanimity
Your legacy will live on forever and ever;
Dalibhunga.

It is in your honour that I pen this elegy
Tata Madiba

Incarcerated for 27 years, yet you had a reservoir of
forgiveness, unencumbered.

Yours was not a struggle in vain
Yours was a struggle like Mose's to gain
The deliverance your people
From cruelty, bondage, subjugation and repression
To Freedom and Uhuru.

You taught us ubuntu
Humanity, sacrifice and compassion
You shaped the world into a place of hope
Like the sun, you shed light where there was darkness
You bestowed passion on humanity
Your footprint cannot be replicated
Till, on the 5th December 2013,
You departed to a new world
Ndiyabulela Madiba!

A great statesman and leader par excellence
For you we mourn…
A short 95 years.
Rest in peace.

SLEEP

Sleep you are a nurse
      So sweet,
Tender, charming and soothing

You massage the sick,
Console
      The less fortunate,
            the destitute,
                  the disadvantaged…
You are inclusive and benefit all

You heal mortal wounds,
      You nurture dreams,
            Sweet, sweet dreams…
You cut short horrid, illusive dreams (that's a plume in your cap)
Slumber…you are faultless, excellent
      Even the Drunk has a passion for you…

Sleep, you have Job's patience, and Solomon's wisdom.
Like the babe and the suckling,
You remain

aloof,

Elevated, majestic and

grandiose.

Mengiliso – The City

This is the story about the long journey,

The long journey to the Great City of Mengiliso

The medieval City of the Imagination,

It's a long way walking to Mengiliso the Lovely City…

The journey takes you through rocky, dusty roads, the rugged

mountains ruled

by baboons, the spotless Zebra, Beasts like Tontons

Maucoute and Fearless Malice!

You will see the cheerless cheaters and cheetahs…the skinny

lions, the marauding elephants, the shameless wife beater, the

dry dams, the singing birds, the honking motorist and the

stinging bees and their lovely, gorgeous honey.

The Parrot asked: 'Mengiliso, what do have in store for the

next generations…

Skinny citizens of this island which you preside over?

Unashamedly.

What type of Democracy?'

The Dove shouted, 'Democracy is only available in Heaven.

Heaven is on Earth'.

So is Mengiliso the Lovely City.

Mengiliso. Genesis. Exodus. Jeremiah. Nehanda.

Nyakasikana. – The Books I really loved to read.

To regurgitate…

To recite…

To sing along if I could.

Besides…If I was the Head of a non-existent school, I did make these compulsory readings!

Especially Mengiliso.

The President must act.

For the citizens deserve better.

LIFE – The Gloomy Side

Life you are a solemn farce

transient and relentless.

Life you are abstract

Subtle and rude

Life you are ambiguous, falsifying and mystifying.

Life you are oblique, gloomy and dark.

Life you are a Greek Gift unrewarding and meaningless.

Life you are foredoomed

Hollow, blunt and DEAD

As in dust to dust.

LIFE – The Sunny Side

Life, dear GOD-GIVEN LIFE

You seem to me 'everything-packed'

I search and search for your essence

I look around

I see misery juxtaposed with happiness; riches with poverty;

The truth with falsehoods, reality with pretense.

What a kaleidoscope!

I still search and search sometimes I feel….

Its like a grope in the dark

But still, life you're wonderful

For you possess copious joy, love and most of all happiness

in abundance, despite!

It is all life in the sunshine.

To Sir Without Love

Dear Death

You steal our breath

How could you be so scary, gloomy…

And a complete stench?

As you bring rot and decay

Its all rivers of tears and blood.

Avenues of sad memories, melancholy…

Broken hearts, misery…Condolences.

Tunnels of darkness, Uncertainty.

Truly yours in sadness

Life incorporated.

When I Think Back

When I think back....
Back into the long forgotten past.
My heart palpitates in a sing song fashion.

Fear creeps over me...
Like the sound of ding-dong bells from the chapel
overwhelming
The silent winter night.

Occasionally a cool wind,
When I think back,
Carries my keener memories into the world far beyond - the
world of the Mysterious and Unknown.
Therein my fear becomes superstitious.
I shudder and tremble as I relapse into the present.
Alas, before me, perched on a tree outside my hut is an owl.

Love

In the paradox
The ones you love are the ones who do not love you.
The ones you do not love are the ones who love you.

Love was, once upon a time, transformed into lust
And lust into love through perseverance and patience
Drawing a thin line between love and lust.

To love your enemy
To love your neighbour
To love yourself
In the paradoxes of love and hate;
Love can turn into hate;
Hate into love!
If you try!
The invisible and invincible power of love
One love. Their Love. Your love. My love.

The Life Beyond

With full respect to the life beyond
I salute all the souls, spirits that lived before my times

Our great ancestors
We revere you
For the wisdom bestowed
Our trust and respect for you is boundless.

Your protection is cherished always.
As you navigate for us and with us
Through life
In our travels and journeys.
Your presence is universal.

You are our compass
Moral and Ethical One.
The foundation is solid.
Our culture and our heritage are flagship.
All because of you.
I submit to you.
The life beyond.
My ancestors.

I salute you.

Tribute.

Dinosaurs of the Present

Re-visit - the dinosaurs of the Jurassic days to know the
present;
Where were you at that crucial moment?
The Slavery, and economic enslavement continues, unabated
But the equality of Man-on earth is necessary.
For how long shall we fight for it?
We shed our skins and remain skeletons as the soul moves on
into the present.
A reincarnation.
Once again of discrimination, wherever we go.
It cannot be right.
For how long?

For those who cry foul
Become the enemies.
For how long
Shall we allow the perilous dinosaurs of the present to reign?
The vestiges of slavery are a shame and ignominy.

Where were you the ancestors when your children were taken
to the Americas to be enslaved?
Where were you?

We know you fought and were subjugated.

It is this generation that has to win the fight for equality.

For we demand equality today.

For equality is an obvious indivisible virtue for all human beings.

Be there at the crucial moment - of total liberation.

Time

Time flies, like Peregrine Falcon

It is already twenty-four years ago.

Time flies.

Does that mean time has wings

Like a bird of a feather?

No. Time moves.

If time moves,

Does that mean time has got wheels like Uncle Chris' scotch-cart?

Or legs like man on earth?

Tick-tick time ticks away.

Time time.

Does time forgive for the wrongs done in the past?

Time time.

Can you stop time for a minute?

A minute is 'all time'.

Time flies.

Timelessness.

We do not have time in this world.

Time time!

Make the best of it

Be happy

Hashtag time!

Little One

Pomp, merriment unbounded
When you came into this world.
Unable to say a word.
Everything appeared as (ab)normal.

But cry you did cry little one.
To herald your arrival into the illusion.

Pure, innocent and defenceless
You entered into earth-senseless
Of hypocrisy, corruption, theft, deception and treachery.
This pseudo-paradise.

(Un)Just Causes

She could kill in the name of God
He could kill for blasphemy

She could kill for love
He could kill in the name of the Devil

She could kill for power
He could kill for justice

She could kill for her human rights
He could kill in the name of culture

What about the sanctity of life!
Why kill for a just cause?
Your Most Highness, be the judge.

I Did Not Choose

Love and respect is all we need.

I am not inferior to anyone.
I am also not superior to anyone.

I did not choose my cultural group
I do not see any benefits, material or otherwise, accruing to
me because of my cultural group
It was not achieved through my own effort.
I cannot change it.

I value my culture,
I also value other cultures.
I cannot fight for belonging to my cultural group.
I cannot fight for being who I am.

I am human being and a proud African.
Amen.

If It Were My World

If it were my world, there will be:

No crying

No suffering

No hurricanes

No droughts

No floods

No cyclones

No sickness

No malaria

No wars

No fighting

No stealing

No greed

One father

One mother

True freedom here and true freedom there

True freedom everywhere

One love

And the truth and only the truth

So help me God.

Dying Twice in a Curriculum Vitae

2031   Died after a short illness

2018   Employed (but self-employed)

2001   Was the moment of truth - plain and simple

1999   Awarded the Noble Prize for Everything Nice on
Earth

1995   Became a born-again Christian

1963   That is when everything started

1910   Started Imagining

1909   Died in Action – death violates the right to life

The epithet read:

Bring your heart in your hands
So that I could see your sincerity

Bring your soul also with you
So that I could feel your presence

Pretenders

Don't aspire to be what you are not
Be proud of who you are

Be proud of your human-ness in one-ness

Be proud of this-ness and that-ness that you are
Witness, I am proud of who I am
Nameless.

By anonymous.

Printed in the United States
By Bookmasters